Conquering Death's Sting

Overcoming the Pain of Grief

SHELLY PRYOR DRAKE

Conquering Death's Sting
Overcoming the Pain of Grief

ISBN: 979-8-9929721-1-5

Library of Congress Control Number: 2025907199

Published in the United States by:
Remnant Media Services & Publications
www.rempublish.com April 2025

DEDICATION

To my dearest husband, Horace Drake III, who has always supported me in every endeavor and pushed me to be my best self. I love you!

To the Pryor family, who helped to build my character and loved me unconditionally along the way.

To all the prayer warriors and friends who have prayed with and for me.

PREFACE

This book shares my views on death and how I have been able to live and rise above my pain from losing loved ones. This book shares how I conquered death's sting and how I learned how to live without the burdens that come with it.

The very idea of death seems morbid to most. Yet, we all experience it. I realized that people grieve in so many ways, and most of us take that heavy weight of grief upon ourselves and try to move on with all those feelings of uncertainty.

I know first-hand how it feels after losing my mother, father, five siblings, three brothers-in-law, several aunts, uncles, niece, all my grandparents, a former husband, and a few friends along the way. Yet, I still stand boldly and I want to help others with God's grace stand boldly, too.

Message To My Audience

For everyone who is reading this book, I genuinely believe that you—yes — you, are not reading these pages by chance. I trust that there is something that God wants you to know that will help you overcome the grief that death has caused in your life from losing that loved one.

I pray that God will speak through these words directly to your heart and allow my experiences to help you heal from your pain and cause you to see the light of happiness and contentment in your life, just as He has done for me.

Moving through all the characteristics of grief is not easy, but it can be accomplished. Admitting that you need help is the first step to overcoming your grief, and your decision to read this book proves that fact. So, let's get started!

Also, please know that I may use the Holy Trinity interchangeably as God, Lord, Jesus, and Holy Spirit, as well as various names that describe Jesus.

TABLE OF CONTENTS

1

SEEDS OF
DEVELOPMENT

"I will instruct you and teach you in the way you should go; I will counsel you with my loving eye on you."
- PSALM 32:8 (NIV)

∞

S ometimes, life can throw you so many curve balls that will make you wonder where you're heading. There were times when I found myself feeling in such despair, yet I always tried to hide how I was feeling and continued to press through it all. I can assure you that my life has certainly not been the most desirable, but I'll always remember that I have been given God's grace, mercy, and love for everything I have ever endured.

Somehow, I felt as though I've always known God, but I can't explain or completely understand how I remember talking to God as a child. I believe He spoke to me then and continued to speak to me. As I got older, I realized that I had a gift of helping and encouraging others, and I was always told that I was such a peculiar child, as the old folks say. I carried wisdom beyond my years.

Growing up, my friends even labeled me as the "Mama" of the group. I remember feeling so comfortable hanging around older people. It was also by nature's design because I was the youngest of nine siblings between my parents. So, I was always around my older brothers and sisters, and there were 10 years between me and my next older sibling, Anthony, whom I will talk about in one of the following chapters.

Some people may say I had this mature attitude at a young age because I was around my oldest siblings, but I beg to differ. I knew it was God Almighty; I knew it was a higher power.

Even as a child, I realized that older people were intrigued by my unusual maturity. Case in point: I remember one of my junior high school teachers felt comfortable talking to me about an abusive boyfriend, and I clearly remember giving her advice to leave him and that she was too nice to be with such an awful person. Yes, she left him eventually and later married a nice guy.

Another case in point: I also remember at one of my class reunions, one of my classmates asked me a question. He asked me, "Shelly, come, what are you doing?" I proceeded to tell him what I was doing at the time. He stopped me abruptly and repeated the question, "Shelly, What are you doing?" I looked him directly in his face, and he said, "Shelly, you need to be speaking to the world" at that moment He grabbed me and hugged me so tightly that he was trembling.

As suddenly as he grabbed me, he released the tight hug, and he turned and walked away. He left me speechless, but I had to admit I wasn't that surprised. Just as I mentioned earlier, I always knew that something was going on, something different about me, and my immature young mind couldn't grasp the ideas of what was really happening but, as I got older, I understood more about God's gifts to His believers.

My classmate I spoke of was very dear to me and he has also passed on to the other side.

As I began to utilize my gift of helping others, it allowed me to give people scenarios of their situations and see a different side. Looking back, I know this foreshadowed what was to come. Either way, I pray that God places His anointing on this book to help others cope with that five-letter word DEATH, which most of us wish to avoid.

I could go on and on about various times that I have experienced specific situations where people have reacted to my behavior—whether it was something that I said or did that was unexplainable—such as saying things to people about their situations that there was no way that I could have known. Sometimes, I must admit I was blown away by some things that occurred. And the only thing I could say was, But God!

Now, you have heard about my experiences and many loved ones who have departed from my life. Knowing that I have truly endured heartache and pain throughout the years, not to mention, as I am finishing this book, I've just lost yet another sibling, my dearest brother James, as I will discuss in the following chapter as well. No matter what, I still believe that God is in control. I trust God, and I refuse to allow anything to keep me from His peace—that unexplainable peace. Philippians 4:17 says that you will experience God's peace, which exceeds anything we can understand. His peace will guard your heart and mind as you live in Christ Jesus. Is this not amazing? God said if you live in Him, He will give you peace that surpasses man's understanding. Yes, I've received and will continue to receive it, but you have to ask for it. And I truly believe that if you ask for His peace, He will deliver it unto you!

2

WHAT ABOUT DEATH?

"I consider that our present sufferings are not worth comparing with the glory that will be revealed in us." ROMANS 8:18

∞

This book is not designed to make you feel guilty about grieving or that you should not grieve. John 16:22 says,*"So with you: Now is your time of grief, but I will see you again and you will rejoice, and no one will take away your joy."*

So, why speak of death? Why not talk about it? It certainly is a part of our lives. We are born into this world, we live then die, and, in every case, it applies to everyone. Most of us just don't want to let go, which is a normal and understandable reaction. But the problem lies when we allow ourselves to linger on and on in the feelings of not wanting to let go for so many reasons, and that's when grief takes over and keeps us from moving forward.

This book is designed to help and show you how I have conquered the pain of grief, and you can, too. Also, it shows how we can look at death differently so that we will not have to suffer so badly from the pain of losing our loved ones.

Getting back to the question, why speak about death? Talking about it may help because no one wants to accept it, even though we know it will eventually come our way. Death is final, and there is no way it is reversible unless a miracle occurs and yes I believe in miracles too but We will discuss that in another book.

Please don't take this personal but, death does not care who you are, where you are from, what status you maintain, what race, creed, or color you are, or what religious status you proclaim. It is inevitable. The very idea of death sometimes stuns us into stillness, immobilizing or stopping us from moving forward, not wanting to do anything, not wanting to be around friends and family, or into total isolation, and if you allow these things to occur, it will take over!

The despair and sadness coming from all these feelings are not God's plans for your life. God wants us to live and enjoy the life He has given us. When someone is taken away, you grieve for a period. That's OK, but staying in that place of grief for a long period is not OK. When I experienced the death of my loved ones, I was overwhelmed by emotions. Looking back, I realized that I gained so much from each loss, Especially those involving my immediate family Members. They taught me so much During their lives yet I also received other lessons unknowingly. All I know is that I did the best that I could And with the weight Of all the emotions and feelings I had no other choice but to lean and depend on Jesus. There was no other way!

Keep reading, and I will eventually show you how I did it.

I honestly believe that a person must yield to death to transition. You hear many people say after they have had a near-death experience that, they have seen a bright light. At that moment, I believe our Lord is giving you a choice to come. In Mark 15:37, Jesus cried with a loud voice and gave up the ghost. At that very moment, He yielded to death.

Psalm 73:26 says, *"My flesh and my heart faileth: but God is the strength of my heart, and my portion forever."* As a Christian, I find comfort in knowing that if you live in Jesus Christ, you will reap the benefits once you depart from this earth. Yes, I know this isn't easy, and you may continue asking why did this happen? Why did you leave me? Some may even boldly ask God, "Why did you let this happen to me?"

If you ask anyone why, then why not ask God? In Matthew 27:46 and Mark 15:34, when Jesus was in the ninth hour hanging upon the cross, he asked God, "Why have you forsaken me?" Yes, it is okay, to ask; you may get an answer to your question or questions, but sometimes, you may not.

We must realize that God is a sovereign- God is all-knowing. He knows everything—from the beginning of every situation to its very end. So, don't beat yourself up about God's decisions. Just know that God's love is so very strong for us that He honors requests based on all facts. 2nd Corinthians 5:8 says, *"To be absent from the body is to be present with the Lord."* Therefore, know that as hard as death is to comprehend or accept, there is hope that if you believe in Jesus Christ and His resurrection—meaning that He died and He rose from death—you may have hope of seeing your loved ones again if they died believing in Him also.

Secondly, I believe that God gives healing through death when your loved ones are sick. They become so very tired of the struggle to maintain from one day to the next, one treatment, one surgery, one doctor visit to the next; they get tired. And, if you are the caregiver, you get tired as well, so just know that it is OK to feel this way; you do not have to feel guilty. It is normal to get tired. I believe that your loved one's expression of being tired just may be their way of being like Jesus on the cross—giving up the ghost. What we must do is accept their choice to do so, and that is ok, too.

Death is no doubt one of the most difficult emotional battles that we as humans will ever experience, and it is because we want our loved ones with us. We, as humans, make those vows and commitments to each other. We hope to be together forever, but in reality, we know that we are not to live forever, and things become abnormal when our loved one transitions to the other side, And some of us severely mourn from such a loss.

We mourn when things, feelings, lifelong plans, etc., and answers to certain questions are never settled. It can get unbearable. So, what I did to help myself through the process of pain and grief and the unsettling in my spirit and soul was that I look back to every single death and tried to figure out, "OK, What did I retrieve from this death?" It happened; there's nothing I can do about it, but what positive thing did I receive from each death." I know maybe some of you are saying, "How can you receive or look at death as anything positive for the sake of being happy, living, and moving on, and not getting stuck in all of the pain." I chose to try and receive something positive. I believe that there is a word from the scriptures that will help us through everything in this life. And I think that the word of God gives us stability, so let's talk about what I've learned from my deceased loved ones.

3

LESSONS FROM
THE DECEASED

∞

The experience of the deaths of my immediate family members have provided me with a few golden nuggets to live by. It may seem a little strange, but I found that finding something positive from the negativity of their deaths helped with the process of accepting that my loved ones were no longer physically with me.

It was not an easy process, And as humans we go through emotions, hard times, and a whole lot of pain; yet grief is normal. I realized that I had to do something different. The hardship and the loss was too great and I discovered this approach, it has worked for me. Do I think about my mom, dad, brothers and sisters? Of course I do. Sometimes, I still shed tears and feel heavy in my heart, but I don't stay there. I live my life And I don't quit moving forward and I refuse to allow myself to get in a slump and get depressed. Those days are over.

I have learned to shift gears, which allows my spirit to be calmed in my worship and praise to God. Most of what I'll call my golden nuggets were not even identified until I became stronger in my walk with Jesus Christ. I could identify what I received, and I'd like to share my experiences with my loved ones and what I was given from each of them.

First, I'd like to tell you about my earliest experience. It happended when I was about two years old. Now, maybe some people may read this and say two years old! Yeah, well, that's what my mom said as well. There was no way that you could remember anything at that age. But the vivid story of my maternal grandmother's funeral—the details I gave her of that day—were so accurate that she could not believe it.

I was just a kid speaking to my mom about this, and now that I am an adult. I have completely forgotten our conversation—my mother and I. But I remember her saying, "I just don't understand how you could remember that day when you were only two years old." How ironic is it that God would give me the gift of becoming an author, and now, I'm writing a book about death and overcoming the grief from it, and that's my earliest memory about death.

Without a doubt, I have had my share of the sting of death. At the age of 11, I lost my brother, Anthony. I am the youngest of all my siblings, and he was 10 years older than me. He was supposed to be the baby of the family, but I made a grand arrival and ended that show! I even entered the world in a particular way. My mother didn't know that she was pregnant with me until 10 days before she had me. So, when I say I made a grand arrival, I did!

I remember my brother Anthony being one of my playmates and my friend. He always had time for me, and I remember that clearly.

But Anthony died a tragic death. He accidentally drowned and was suddenly taken away from our family on the 4th of July, 1978. Anthony's drowning devastated my entire family because it happened so suddenly. It was my first experience with death and the pain that surrounded it.

But there's more. This was the second time I remember hearing the voice of the Lord. Before Anthony left the house, I followed his every footstep because I was upset that he was leaving, and I wanted to go too, but I couldn't. As he got in the car and drove away, the voice of the Lord said to me, "You didn't say goodbye to him."

Of course, I didn't know what that meant until we were informed of his death later that day. As a kid, people think you don't understand, but I knew what was happening.

My brother's death was also the first time I experienced grief and longing! As a child, I really couldn't understand what I was feeling, but as I got older, I was aware of that feeling of numbness; I knew there was something to it. Of course, I couldn't explain it, but as I look back, I can now. As I mentioned, I was an unusual child. Although I can't remember all the details, I was very aware of all the emotions of my family members, especially my mother. I grew up in church. That's where my mom always took us, and every time I saw her cry at church, I always felt as a child that she was crying and missing my brother. And that felt as though she never truly healed from her grief from losing her youngest son.

As a kid, I was going through the motions, and as I look back, I can see God's hand in it and the numbness I've felt throughout the years. I'm sure God gave me that same feeling, His peace.

Now, the golden nugget I received from Anthony's death is:

Some relationships are not meant to last.
And you have to learn how to cope and
move on without them.

Fast forward to 1986, July 14th, 1986 to be exact. I moved away from home to Atlanta, GA, to live with a couple of great friends, Yvette and Sherry. I felt as though I was living my best life. My mom and I would speak nearly every day, and things were going great. I got a couple of jobs and was in school; life was wonderful. But on October 30th, 1986, my whole world changed. My beloved mother, Rutha, passed away. Now, my mom was truly the best mother ever to walk the face of this earth. She was a woman of God and virtue. She was a woman of few words and very humble, but every statement she made was packed with power.

She loved her family unconditionally. This experience of losing my mom was on another level because when Mama is gone, you have to pull it together and realize that you are all grown up, or at least you need to be.

My mother's death left me in a state of disbelief. I said to myself, "Here I go again;" although a few years had passed since my brother's death, and I found myself just going through the motions, this experience was like no other.

The pain was so deep that I felt as though I was having an out-of-body experience of some kind. I know I lived through every day, yet I didn't remember much about anything. I don't even remember much else about the day of the funeral or the days before it. But, about two weeks after my mother's funeral, I had a dream about my mom, and she was radiant. She had a heavenly glow; she was sitting in this beautiful bed. And nothing looked familiar. Everything was just brilliant! Then my mother told me, "Shelly, I'm ok." In the dream, I began to cry. And I woke up.

Remembering my dream vividly, I began to cry hysterically. This cry was a cry of relief. After crying for a while, I felt I needed to have that experience so I could truly let go. I felt that God gave me exactly what I needed to move forward. You see, the day that my mom died, she called me. I had gone to a doctor's appointment with a friend and missed her call. I felt guilty for not being there, not knowing what my mom had to say to me. But, whatever it was, it wasn't meant for me to hear, and that's how I had to accept that I missed her call.

Yes, I could have allowed it to get in the way and pondered what she had to say to me, but I chose to receive the message from my mother in the dream that she was ok.

The golden nuggets I received from my mother are too many to count, but the main ones are:

Stay humble and true to yourself. Most of all, love yourself. Also, you don't need many friends, just a few good ones.

I say that because I only remember one friend of my mother who would visit often, and that was it. If there was ever anyone else in her presence, especially around home, it was family. Also, she'll always say;

Cherish your husband and be committed.

She was undeniably a devoted wife. Yes, closure is what I needed, and I truly thank God for giving it to me. When I think of my mother, I feel she is present with the Lord. And there was no doubt in my mind that that short five-foot-two-inch little powerhouse of a woman is with our Lord and Savior, Jesus Christ, the Almighty King!

The next death that occurred was 11 years later, and after my mother's death, my father, Arthur (Shag), died. My dad and I started our relationship on shaky ground. I loved my father; he was a good person and, most of all, a man of his word. After my mom died, my dad and I grew closer. He would tell me stories about his childhood and give me fatherly advice as any good father would. Daddy succumbed to his death in 1997. But before his death, I was able to lead him to Christ, which was one of my greatest achievements ever. I was heavily involved in the church at the time. God allowed me to ask my father if he believed that Jesus Christ was his Lord and Savior, that Jesus died on the cross for his sins, and that if he died, he was saved. He received Christ that day; yes, my father was born again.

I remember the weekend before my father passed, I came home because he wasn't feeling well, and when he realized I had made it to the house, my dad did not want me out of his sight. If I left his sight, he would tap his cane on the floor. Therefore, I was at his beck and call.

After I served his dinner, I got him ready for bed. After about 30 minutes or so, he fell asleep. Well, that meant I could sleep, so I dressed for bed and went to sleep. As I fell asleep, I dreamed of my father standing at my bedroom doorway. I looked up at him; he looked young and handsome, like he had not been sick. I didn't think much about the dream as everyone slept through the night. The next day, I remember having another good day with Dad, and that was on Sunday, and I went home after visiting him that weekend. Daddy died the following Thursday.

I was devastated from losing my father; now, I was without both of my parents. I was crushed as I would no longer hear his laughter and jokes. Although I was devastated for a short while, God never disappoints. I asked for His peace and received it. I was grateful to God that I didn't take anything to heart for my dad because of the things that I didn't understand as a child. I appreciate that God gave me time to see my father's heart and to know that my dad loved me, and I loved my dad like a baby girl should. Most of all, I know that he loved God in the end. The golden nugget I received from my father is that:

You should never judge a book by its cover.

Some things occurred in my father's childhood that should never have happened. I always thought my father was mean, but he was just a man who meant what he said, and I'm so much like him. My father also taught me to:

Say what you mean and mean what you say.

That statement needs no explanation; it's as plain as it gets!

I have three words: Bertha Lee Pryor, my beloved sister. This woman was my best friend until she left this world. I have yet to meet anyone like her, and she portrays strength like no other. She was brutally honest and had the biggest heart ever for our family. She was the real deal, and she disliked anyone fake. She was strong in her faith, like Mama. She believed that Jesus would always make way for her in every life endeavor as she would walk it out no matter what. She was about action!

In James 2:14-26, the scriptures speak about faith without works, and she lived these scriptures throughout her life. She was the backbone for me and many others in our family, but I believe God allowed Bertha to be an example for me to follow.

Like my mother, she didn't have many friends, and neither do I. If she said it like my father, you can expect it. So do I. She was about business. She taught me how to dress and act like a lady and, most of all, to be about God's word and honor it. She was my go-to since my mom died. When my sister got sick, God gave me His strength and power to help take care of her along with her son, Tracy, and other family members pitched in. It was a hard time because it was so hard seeing her deteriorate from such a strong posture to a weak vessel, not to mention that, at the time, my former husband was sick as well. I had to take care of them and work a full-time job. Now, I can tell you that there was no way in my power that I could have done this without my Lord and Savior, Jesus Christ.

There are so many things I've learned from my sister, but the golden nuggets that I've taken away from her, just like my mom's, are too many to count. I can honestly say that out of all that she had helped me through, I received two main golden nuggets from Bertha. And that is:

Being honest. Although honesty hurts sometimes, still, things will work out no matter what when you tell the truth!

And the second golden nugget I received from my dear sister, Bert, which was her nickname is:

Be about your business! Don't expect anybody to do anything for you when you know you need to get things done!

The death of my oldest brother, George, was senseless. And this was another time of just going through the motions. I had to ask God for His peace because I did not understand.

His death was a hard pill to swallow. My brother was a lot like my dad. He was so darn funny. George led a very frugal lifestyle. he didn't believe in just buying anything. He believed that eating a home cooked meal was better than going out any day and he was a great cook. He was kind; he never hurt my feelings. He loved his baby sister, and that I knew. One thing about my brother George: when he wanted you to be aware of something, he would always say something to make you think or ask you why. George was family-oriented, and he loved us wholeheartedly.

A few days before George died, he asked me to take him to his favorite store. We were conversing about how people would sometimes tell lies on you and for some reason that stuck with me so I can say the Golden Nugget that I received from my brother George was that you must always:

Rise above the lies!

When people lie to you, as long as God knows the truth, that is the only one who matters. And that's the golden nugget that I received from my brother George.

The next person who died in my immediate family was my oldest sister. I can't deny that the women in my family are women who have strong faith. My older sister, Eula Mae, was my go-to person after my sister Bert passed. She had her own family, so as a child, I wasn't so close to her, but as I got older, I called and talked to her more, and I got to know her better.

What I learned about my sister was that she was so much like my mom, a woman with strong prayer, and faith, someone who knew how to get a prayer through, and every time I needed to talk to her or I was going through something or having issues on my job or whatever the problem may have been, Whatever the problem may have been, she knew I would never try to make trouble. She always touched and agreed with me and prayed for me through certain situations; I'll forever be grateful for that. The golden nugget I received from my sister, Eula Mae, is:

Prayer changes things!

I don't care what you're going through. If you honor Christ Jesus, pray in Jesus' name, and believe in your heart that you will receive what you prayed for, then I believe it will be given unto you So therefore you must understand that God knows everything.

As I stated before, He is a sovereign God. You can't think He doesn't know everything, so if your prayers aren't answered for whatever reason, I truly believe it is for our good.

Now, the next death that occurred was an epic loss, which occurred about a year and three months after my eldest brother died. I can't begin to tell you how devastating the loss of my former husband, Ray felt.

Ray and I were married for fifteen years. Although our marriage was not perfect, we were devoted to each other. Ray was not saved when I met him and he liked to hang out a lot! There were challenging times because of this but, through it all we made it work because we wanted it to. I must admit I felt deprived of his time and I was very disappointed that we could've spent more moments together. Now, he was so sick yet there was nothing I could do about the situation but pray and plead with God to help us both.

Overall we shared a good life together; our love was strong. I feel like he would have done anything in this world to make me happy. He was extremely handsome and had an absolutely beautiful smile.

I gave our marriage all of myself. I cherished Ray just as my mother cherished my father. I quit my job to be his caregiver. Like my father while Ray was suffering with his illnesses I led him to Christ. I knew if anything happened such as death, That he would be OK because he would be with Christ. Also The day of Ray's funeral his best friend Aaron spoke and he gave the testimony that He saw his friend change and that he had no doubt that Ray was saved by God's grace. My heart was filled with joy and during his funeral service I began to praise the Lord. I know that some people viewed my praise as something that was odd but people should not judge you when they truly don't know your story or have never been in this type of situation.

Aaron's testimony meant more to me than any one could ever imagine. Ray's Heart was massive and He deserved to be with Christ Jesus. Ray was family oriented; and we spent much time with our family. He was an excellent cook, and many times, we would have huge cookouts and feed 50 to 100 people. Losing him was a tragedy, to say the least. I knew Ray was sick, but I didn't want to accept the fact that I could lose him to death. And when it occurred, I felt like his death had pulled the bottom from under my feet. I don't know what dying feels like, but if I had to explain it, I can say I felt like I was dying, too.

God said in His word that when you make your wedding vows, He makes two become one, and two becoming one in the spirit realm is a powerful union; this is the only relationship where God proclaims in His word to make two spirits join as one. And the separation of this relationship by death contains an enormous amount of pain. It makes you wonder if I can bear such a heavy burden; I asked myself, "What are you doing, Shelly? What will you do without the other part of you no longer being here?" Ray had not just gone away somewhere, but he was gone away from this earth forever! I thought I was losing my mind! This pain was so unbearable that I felt like every emotion from every previous death was rolled into one.

During every hospital stay, I was there, and there wasn't anything I wouldn't do and I didn't do, so guilt was never an issue for me after he passed. I just missed him dearly. About three weeks after Ray's funeral, I visited the grave site. On this particular day, I was having a horrible day. I couldn't stop crying; I don't even remember the drive to the grave site. I got out of the car, and I just stood by his grave site, and I started sobbing horribly, and at that very moment, I begged for God's peace. And God came and rescued me. And I thank God He did because I was spiraling downward fast. The Golden Nuggets That I received from Ray was: **other than God-family first.** The second Golden Nugget that I received from Ray was **Devotion- dedication , love and commitment meant everything to us both!**

The last death I will discuss is my brother James, and as I am writing this book, my brother James died. He was the last brother born between my parents. Being shocked and dismayed is nothing short of how I felt. In the beginning, when I heard the news that he had passed, I was in total disbelief. I spoke with him about two and a half hours before receiving the news.

The last words that my brother said to me were, "Shelly, everything's going to be alright," but losing him is certainly not OK; it wasn't alright.

It may sound odd, but I immediately felt lonely. I felt this way because I viewed my brother as our family's patriarch; he was our anchor, and his loss left me feeling as though I was falling yet never being caught. I felt myself becoming angry that he was taken away from me because it happened so suddenly. He went into the hospital; the doctors did tests after tests. Then, three weeks later, he died. I was angry! I was devastated, and this death broke my spirit. I didn't want to do anything and for at least three days I didn't. I didn't get out of bed or go to work. I couldn't function, nor could I stop crying. I knew I needed God's peace. I knew I needed spiritual help, and I knew that was the only way for me to get out of this dreadful place.

There's nothing like the peace of God. It is unexplainable. Since I received the peace of God, I can function better. And as each day passed, I felt better. The enemy tried to make me out to be a liar, and he wanted to stop me from writing this book by keeping me in such a grievous state. One thing about death is that it will leave you in a state of confinement, stopping you in your tracks if you allow it to happen. The sting of grief is so powerful that you may feel like you don't want to do anything; you may not want to get out of bed, eat, or anything else, but I promise you that you must choose to get up and rise above the circumstance, and that's what I did.

You must put yourself in a spiritual place and come out of that dark place. The most powerful golden nugget I received from my brother James is:

Always protect what you love.

Even on his deathbed, my brother was still trying to protect me and my feelings. Although at his last moments, I believe he knew something or felt some way when he spoke those last words to me, "Shelly, everything's going to be OK." How honorable is that! My big brother James departed this world, giving me his ultimate protection!

For every feeling of negativity that I felt from my loss, for every tear that I've cried over the years, all the grief and pain have been replaced by the lessons that I received from my loved ones who have transitioned from this side of Earth.

Therefore, I choose to have wonderful memories and remember our love for one another. I also choose to have and receive the Holy Spirit as my comforter to help me cope with this life journey.

4

Where Do I Go From Here?

"So do not fear, for I am with you; do not be dismayed, for I am your God. I will strengthen you and help you; I will uphold you with my righteous right hand."
- ISAIAH 41:10

∞

This sting of death that I am referring to is called "grief," which can be extremely complex. The question is, "Where are you going from here?" Yet, what is here? Well, "*Here*" is your emotional state and how you cope with this difficult situation—that very thing that has a hold of you and will not let go! It is a known fact that everyone grieves differently. The level of its severity depends upon the individual who is suffering from grief, as well as the relationship that was shared with the loved ones whom you lost to death.

Death certainly causes many diverse types of grievous feelings that manifest after such a loss.

Most of us have felt some of these characteristics, and many have felt all of them. Some people experience an excessive amount of anxiety, so they turn to alcohol, overeating and begin to gain lots of weight, which can lead to specific types of illnesses, and this can also lead to taking an excessive amount of medication and other complications that may arise. On the other hand, some people stop eating and lose a lot of weight, which can lead to unhealthy situations. I merely ate to survive. I lost weight because I was not eating properly, and I went from a size 14 to a size 8.

Some people feel an extreme level of sadness with a deep, dreadful feeling of loss and extreme periods of just weeping. Most times, these people will isolate themselves from others, and deep depression may set in and cause suicidal thoughts. Always know that suicide is never a place that God wants for any of us. And as bad as you may feel, you should never consider suicide as an answer to end your grief!

Anger is certainly one of them. I'm so well aware of that frustration, knowing that you can do absolutely nothing to change the situation. As I spoke about earlier with my brother James, I just felt so angry that he was taken away from me. It's normal to feel this way, and that's something that I had to realize.

Some people fear being alone, not knowing what to do, where to go, or their next move. I felt this emotion when my former husband Ray died. I was completely lost and did not know if I would make it. I was confused about what I would do next and where I was going; I just was unsure about anything. I could not sleep, and I was extremely restless. When losing a spouse to death, I do believe that most people who are married can relate to this particular characteristic of grief.

After being intimately close to someone, you may find yourself constantly thinking about that person and unable to focus, make sound decisions, or move forward with daily tasks. I also found myself in this situation where I no longer wanted to live in our shared house without him being there. Therefore, I decided to move away. Shortly thereafter, I regretted moving away, and it felt like I had made that decision too soon because of my status. I realized that God allowed everything to work out for my good.

Guilt is a characteristic that many people feel after losing someone. There is a forever guilt about what they wish they could have done differently with that loved one, that thing you regret not saying or doing that perhaps your loved one requested from you, knowing that so many things were left unfinished or even unaccomplished. What about the things you promised you would do yet never did? The fact that you cannot do anything to change it because the situation just cannot be undone can cause unhealthy stress levels. That can take a whole different turn and now cause physical damage to your body and your mental health, And yes, even death!

I call all these characteristics "heavy burdens." One of my favorite scriptures is Matthew 11:28-30, which states, *"Come unto me, all ye that labor and are heavy laden, and I will give you rest. Take my yoke upon you, and learn of me; for I am meek and lowly in heart: and ye shall find rest unto your souls. For my yoke is easy, and my burden is light."* These scriptures have been medicine for my soul. The weight that I was carrying was most of these characteristics of grief, such as sadness, anger, fear, etc.

At one point, throughout all the deaths that I have experienced, I am sure that I have felt them all. Throughout the years, some of the pain I remember, and some of them I truly don't remember, but based on what I have experienced from grieving, being a believer in Jesus Christ. He made an offer to take my heavy burdens, and that was an offer that I just could not refuse! Now, there are two other characteristics I would like to discuss, and I see the brighter side of these characteristics because they give something positive to such a negative circumstance.

The first one is numbness, which feels like you are just going through the motions and not feeling pain or anything, feeling detached from what you know that you are going through. As I was going through each death throughout the years, I remember just going through the motions. I relate this to God's peace. He detaches your mental state of grief and pain and allows you to be at peace by not having to entertain those feelings that grief causes. God said that His peace is unexplainable, and I have experienced this type of peace, which I will discuss later in detail in the following chapters.

The last characteristic related to grief is "relief." Most people do not want to discuss this characteristic or will not admit to having felt it in this manner because some people may tend to shun someone who feels relief when a person dies. But I believe there is a sense of peace embedded in this characteristic. For instance, if you ever had a loved one who was extremely sick and had gone through a long traumatic suffering, it is normal for a person to feel relief when a person dies in this manner.I experienced this feeling of relief with my sister, Bertha, and my former husband, Ray. Neither one of them deserved the suffering that they endured, and since I was a caregiver to them both, it was so hard to see their struggle with illness.

I felt a sense of relief when they passed because I no longer had to see the people that I love dearly suffer so deeply. I clearly remember praying so deeply for their healing, but they still died. Through the years, I have come to the realization that their healing was through their death.

Yes, I do believe that death is healing in some cases, such as these. No matter how you handle grief, it is something you can conquer. Also, I will reiterate that it is normal to grieve, and yes, the timeline varies for grieving; for some people, it takes a longer time than others to overcome, but there is a way of escape. Please don't get me wrong; I'm not telling you to give up your memories or that you can't cry or miss your loved ones. Those feelings are probably never going to go away, but what I am telling you is that when you have been grieving for years. It has negatively impacted your normal way of living. That's when grieving has become detrimental to you. Knowing that grief is very painful and grief can cause all types of issues for you, even death! So, do you want to be relieved from your grieving state? Some people grieve for years and don't know how to let go, and I want to help.

Do you think your loved ones want you to grieve for them like you're grieving? Probably not! I suggest to seek God's plans for your life. In addition to receiving God's help through reading and believing in His word, some people may need to speak to a spiritual or mental health counselor. These are options for you to get help. Yes, I have experienced both, and for me personally, what helped me is taking the time to get to know Jesus and receive the help that the Holy Spirit has to offer me. Whatever you decide, move out of your own way and allow God to provide His way for you. *"Cast all your anxiety on Him because He cares for you."* – 1 Peter 5:7.

5

FOLLOW
GOD'S PLAN

"Trust in the Lord with all your heart and lean not on your own understanding; in all your ways submit to Him, and He will make your paths straight."
- PROVERBS 3:5-6 (NIV)

∞

After discussing all of the characteristics of grief and the pain of losing a loved one to death, it is high time to stop trying to do it your way and allow God to help you follow his plan for your life. Now is the time to focus on the help you need to get to the next stages of your life. Having walked this walk so many times, I believe that because of my Christian walk, first and foremost, I turned my focus to the word of God. The first scripture that comes to mind is Psalms 121: 1-2, which states, *"I will look to the hills for which cometh my health. All my help comes from the Lord, the maker of Heaven and Earth."*

These scriptures are short and sweet and yet so powerful! God said not some, but all of your help will come from me—if you indeed seek my help. Now, that sounds like a sure plan to me! It's one that I have followed and saved my life. Let's make it clear: God does not want you to live a life running in circles because of what you have lost, and He doesn't want you to live a life of misery because you miss that loved one. God doesn't want you to carry guilt around for the rest of your life because of a missed moment!

Our Lord and Savior wants us to depend upon Him, so why not try Him at His word. God will not disappoint you! How do you give all you have felt to Jesus throughout the years? All you have to do is ask! It's just that simple. God isn't complicated. He will honor what He has said in His word. Some of you may ask, why ask God because he should already know what I need. Yes, He knows what we need. God is omniscient. He knows the past, present, and future, but the choice to receive His peace and plan for our lives is a choice we must believe and receive.

In Matthew 7:7, Jesus states, *"Ask, and it will be given to you; seek, and you will find; knock, and the door will be open to you."* The scripture in Matthew is also another powerful short scripture, and it is very clear! God wants us to come to Him if we are in need, ask Him to deliver us from our agony, and set us on a renewed path after suffering a loss.

Before I go any further, you must desire and accept something before God's plan for your life is activated. You must believe in Jesus Christ, and you must believe that Jesus Christ died on the cross, and we must believe in his death and resurrection, and that we rose with Him, and we are saved by the blood that He shed on the cross for our sins. Once you have accepted Jesus into your heart and established a covenant with Him, He will begin to work on your behalf. Several fringe benefits come with accepting Jesus Christ!

We'll discuss more about this in the upcoming chapters. But most of all, you will receive His unconditional love. God's very name means love. He truly loves us because He created us. The type of love the Lord has for us is personal; He's compassionate about us, and His love for us has no boundaries. God's sacrificial love for us is so powerful that the very reason that Jesus died on the cross was for us to have life. His love is beyond human comprehension. When you truly understand that God's love accepts you with open arms as you are, you realize He only wants the best for us all. So, no matter what you were feeling toward him when He allowed your loved ones to be taken away, whether you were angry with Him or you distanced yourself from Him, none of that matters when you choose to accept him. God is not like man. Matthew 5:4 says, *"Blessed are those who mourn, for they will be comforted."* What a wonderful God we serve!

What is God's plan? Jeremiah 29: 11-12 states, *"For I know the plans I have for you, declares the Lord, plans to prosper you and not to harm you, plans to give you hope and a future. Then you will call on me and come and pray to me, and I will listen to you."* Every time I read these particular scriptures, it just makes me happy because God clearly says that He has specific plans for His followers, His people's plans of goodness and no harm! These scriptures truly helped me during the time that I experienced the death of my loved ones. Although I did suffer for a while, accepting God's plan and His promises allowed me to move forward and not stay in that negative place.

Turn to God's word in prayer and supplication when things happen, such as a loved one dying initially; yes, it will probably knock you down. And yes, you may struggle with your emotions, shock, and pain. However, the promises of God are strong, powerful, and, most of all, true. If you trust in Him wholeheartedly and believe in the words that He has given us all, everything will work out for you.

There are things you may not understand when some situations occur, but as I said earlier, Our Lord and Savior Jesus Christ will not fail. Truly getting to know God is the next step. Allow Him to be your friend!

6

SEIZING TIME WITH GOD TO MEDITATE

"Be still, and know that I am God; I will be exalted among the nations, I will be exalted in the earth." - PSALM 46:10

∞

I am in awe of His goodness after all that Jesus has done for me. Despite all my loss from family and friends, I am a living witness to God's kindness towards me. I'm the first to admit that grief is not easy to overcome, but with His help, I have survived because I have decided to follow His guidance. Although I still struggle, I turn to God And when I feel a situation is trying to defeat me He is the only answer.

Seizing time with God to meditate is an important step in healing and maintaining stability in your life after much sorrow. Learning and understanding that God has love for us, the benefits of spending time and meditating, and the words of Jesus Christ can only strengthen your faith in Him, believing that your breakthrough is coming even though it hasn't arrived. Love on Jesus, and Let Jesus love on you!

Let Him love you to the place of pure joy and peace! I can promise you that there's nothing like it! Jesus makes you feel special, and you can't do anything but be thankful to Him. It makes you want to build that strong personal relationship with God.

Therefore, indulge in the Lord Jesus and His promises for you, and praise Him continuously. When I say praise Him continuously, it can be as subtle as saying, "Thank you, Jesus." It could be as simple as thanking God that you finally stopped crying over your situations, or maybe even the fact that you don't feel guilty anymore because of your loved one's death.

Seizing time with the Lord and understanding Him will transform you from sadness, pain, and grief to strength, love, and power. Getting to know God is one of the most important things that you will accomplish in your life. As I stated earlier, God is love; His name is love, so to me, it's clear that's what He wants to offer to those of us who truly believe in Him. God is Holy, meaning He is set apart from sin, pure, perfect in every way, and sacred! What does God have to offer when you spend time with Him?

As I mentioned in a previous chapter, you will receive fringe benefits because my God has so many, and He wants to give them to us freely. One of God's major fringe benefits is undoubtedly His love. In addition to that powerful love, He wants an intimate relationship with us. How awesome is that!

There is nothing for me to sit down and have a whole conversation with God as though He's sitting right next to me. Some of you may think that's odd, but that's the relationship He wants to have with us.

Remember early on when I stated that I've always felt like I've known God? Therefore, I've been talking to Him for a long time, and have continued to have that personal relationship with him.

Seizing time with God builds a personal relationship, especially now when you know that you need His healing power to deliver you; also, to maintain that intimate relationship with our Lord and Savior Jesus Christ, allowing Him to give His peace. As I've stated earlier, asking for God's peace is something I ask for often, and it has helped me tremendously. His peace is truly unexplainable, and as I stated earlier, it reminds me of the characteristic of numbness now. I've explained this in the previous chapter, but there are no words for it other than total calmness!

With all the challenges you've had to endure trying to see your way through all the fog and uncertainties of your next move, I suggest you ask for His PEACE, believe in your heart that you have received it, and try your best to rest in a calming state of mind. You will certainly see a difference in your circumstances.

Next, two other fringe benefits of God are His strength and power. When you spend time with God, He will give you strength and power. The more time you spend with Him, the more strength and power you will receive. No matter what comes your way, you will start to overcome the challenges in your life. You will begin to believe in yourself and realize that you are strong enough to handle any situation that you're in.

Because of God's strength and power, I am now writing this book and reflecting on how I have learned to move forward without getting stuck in a place of despair. The next fringe benefit that God gives His believers is protection. I don't know of anyone who doesn't want to be protected. What does protection from God look like?

When you meditate on His word, He will guide you throughout life and not allow you to stumble. Now, I know a lot of you may read this and say well, "God didn't protect me from being harmed by someone. God didn't protect me when my loved ones died." Well, I'm going to say that we can't blame everything on God—some things we have to be held accountable for.

We often get used to doing anything and everything we want to do, and then we want God to rescue us from it all. I usually refer to the Bible and basic instructions for living every day. I know it is to receive any blessing from the Lord, particularly the topic at hand: protection. He wants us to follow His instructions So that He can freely give us His security.

A favorite scripture portraying God's protection is Isaiah 52:12: *"For ye shall not go out with haste, nor go by flight: for the LORD will go before you, and the God of Israel will be your reward."*

God simply says He will go before you, make the path straight, and protect you from behind. What an almighty God I serve!

Lastly, there are two other fringe benefits that I wish to speak about. They are called mercy and grace! Now, these two are mega fringe benefits! God loves us so much that even when we spiral out of control, go in the wrong direction, or make a devastating decision that could alter our entire lives, God will give us His mercy and His grace so our situation may suddenly change and reverse.

I just experienced God's mercy and grace being given to me when I lost my brother, James, in November of 2024. And I must admit that throughout my life as a whole, He has given me more than my share.

I am grateful, but getting back to my brother's death because it's so fresh, I mentioned that I was angry. And my anger was toward God. I know some people will read this, and they will truly relate. Some will probably think this is the most despicable thing ever, but my transparency will not allow me to lie. The truth shall set you free; this is what John 8:32 says.

When I came to my senses a few days later, I knew I had to repent to our Lord and Savior, Jesus Christ, and ask for His forgiveness and peace. God gave me His mercy and grace despite the negative feelings that I carry toward Him for allowing my brother to die. God did not have to allow me to be at peace, but I asked for His peace and love toward me because I chose to surrender. It's so powerful, and I repented with a clear heart. God, in turn, gave me His gifts of mercy and grace!

It is so important to follow Christ at this time in your life. Receive all that is good from Him, and you will know what to receive when you take it upon yourself. Read and meditate on all His promises. Allow His love and gifts to manifest in your lives, and try Jesus at His word. Therefore, you should find the time to spend with God and pray to Him. Always ask for His guidance on everything that you do.

Continue to ask for His peace upon you so that when you have memories of your loved ones on birthdays and Christmas holidays, you feel better. Remember, it is okay to have these memories. But what's not okay is when you decide to stay there. The Lord has too much to offer to us to set us free, and we should be so grateful that He has truly given us a way of escape.

Therefore, it is time to let go for good!

7

LETTING GO
FOR GOOD

"So do not fear, for I am with you; do not be dismayed, for I am your God. I will strengthen you and help you; I will uphold you with my righteous right hand."
- ISAIAH 41:10

∞

You may ask yourself, "After all I have gone through, how do I let go for good?" Letting go for good is not forgetting the memories of your loved ones but is a way for you to cope with physically living without them. It also doesn't mean, to never think about them, talk about them, and never cry for them again; as a human, that is impossible, but you can let go of how you handle losing a loved one. You can also establish a way to deal with it positively, which benefits you.

I have found that the word of God does it for me. I get total joy just thinking about His promises. And sometimes, God's deliverances may not come when I want them to, but they come when I need them most. Whatever your outlet is, remember that you need to release your pain, I challenge you to write down your thoughts I believe it will help. The most profound outlet is Jesus Christ, for there's nothing like Him.

I have a couple of favorite scriptures that will explain in more detail why you should take an interest in God's word. God's word can help you let go for good, and to let go in the manner in which I'm speaking, you must trust God Wholeheartedly.

Proverbs 3: 5-6 states, *"Trust in the Lord with all your heart and lean not unto your own understanding. In all your ways, acknowledge him, and he shall direct your path."*

Every single thing that you've endured: the hurt, the sleepless nights, the deep pain that you felt, that sickness that you may have endured, the confusion, the loneliness, the periods where you isolated yourself, the overeating, or the times when you wouldn't eat anything, or times where you didn't know what your next move would be, God knew it all; He saw everything that you went through. And He wants us all to trust Him no matter what.

Not only did He say trust me, but trust me with all your heart and lean not unto your understanding. Now, with everything we endured, we tried to find a solution. We wanted to make it on our own, yet we often found ourselves stuck where we couldn't endure the hurt.

However, I believe this scripture is telling us the keys to truly letting go and allowing God to take control to save us from the dreadful feelings of grief.

He says, "Acknowledge me in all thy ways and He will direct our path." How do we acknowledge God or let Him know when we're feeling the characteristics of grief, while barely hanging on? With prayer and supplication, we go to our Lord and Savior, Jesus Christ, and tell him everything! This is what He wants from us; He wants an intimate relationship. Therefore, He wants us to come to Him, and tell him all about our troubles.

But, you have to establish a relationship with God, an intimate relationship with Him, and you have to acknowledge that He's sovereign; He has control of everything. Therefore, by giving your worries, pain, fears, and confusion when you let go and let God take control, you will allow your trust to grow in Him. God knows everything; you must believe and have faith in Him that when you request His strength, love, and guidance through prayer, He will answer you. We must make a sound commitment, obey His words, and follow His divine plan for our lives because His plans are higher than ours. *ISAIAH 55:8-9 For my thoughts Are not your thoughts come neither Are your ways my ways, declares the Lord As the heavens are higher than the Earth so are my ways higher than your ways and my thoughts higher than your thoughts*

Trusting in God is the most satisfying action a person can do for themselves and their spiritual growth. These scriptures are His divine words, and I found that praying God's words back to Him brings you deliverance. This means that if you quote his scriptures back to Him and believe that you will receive what that scripture says or what that scripture is telling you to do, He will honor your requests because His words have total truth.

Even if you do not have the strongest faith in the world, the scriptures say that the size of a mustard seed of faith will deliver results to your prayer requests, as in *Matthew 17:20 "He replied, 'Because you have so little faith. Truly I tell you, if you have faith as small as a mustard seed, you can say to this mountain, 'Move from here to there,' and it will move. Nothing will be impossible for you.'"*. If God doesn't answer your prayers, there is a reason; but if you ask for Him to reveal why the prayer wasn't answered. I believe He will show you that, too. He desires to comfort and help you conquer the sting of death!

CONCLUSION

Everything I have said throughout this book, if there is nothing else I want to portray, is that I hope that I have set an example that I have submitted to God, that I have allowed Him to take away my pain and agony from grief, that I have tried and sometimes failed to obey His word. Still, the key point is that whenever I have strayed, I have chosen to get back on the path of righteousness.

I trust God with my life, allowing him to control it and guide me. I thank God for his protection and his love toward me. My faith is strong in Jesus Christ, and I know I'm not alone. He's with me and very near to me. I hope that the things I have revealed in this book, the golden nuggets, portray that they're gone, and I don't have to forget them. Yet, I don't have to allow their death to put me in a state of not living freely and knowing that my deceased loved ones truly loved me, and I truly believe that they would not want me to live a grievous life longing for them constantly.

The choice is yours. Either you're going to live freely from death's sting of grief and live an abundant life through Jesus Christ Or NOT! My prayer is that my testimony of how I conquered death's sting and overcame the pain from grief will somehow help you do the same. I pray that you choose to live with Jesus Christ!

Selah and Amen!

Thank You for Reading!

If you enjoyed this book, please return to Amazon to leave a review of your reading experience.

I truly appreciate your purchase and the time you took to read this book. My hope and prayer is that it helped you overcome the pain of grief!

With gratitude,

Shelly Pryor Drake

MEET THE AUTHOR

Shelly Pryor Drake

I have never strayed from being true to myself or others. My motto has always been: *"If you don't want to know the truth, don't ask me."* I speak from the heart, especially regarding what I believe and know is right. I've had a profound relationship with God for as long as I can remember. My faith has carried me through life's highest peaks and lowest valleys, including the valley of grief. One of my classmates once told me, *"Shelly, everybody knows that you're religious."* That resonated with me because I follow Jesus Christ and don't make excuses for it. My hope, healing, and strength all come from Him. Grief can shake us at our core, but God, El Shaddai, the Peacemaker, has never left my side. His love has held me together through tears, silence, and breakthrough moments. He called me to write about overcoming *grief,* share my story, and remind others that healing is possible. I pray readers feel seen, understood, and, most importantly, loved with every page. I will always use my voice and this gift of writing to proclaim God's truth and His goodness.